Turkey earthquake

Death toll rises as search and rescue continues

By

Morgan O. Winter

Table of contents

Chapter 5: Providing aid to those affected

- Overview of the efforts by aid organizations and government agencies to provide assistance to those affected by the earthquake
- Discussion of the challenges in providing aid in the aftermath of a disaster

Chapter 6: The recovery process

- Overview of the process of rebuilding after an earthquake
- Discussion of the challenges and obstacles that must be overcome in order to fully recover

Chapter 7: Preparing for future earthquakes

- Explanation of the steps that can be taken to prepare for earthquakes
- Discussion of the importance of earthquake preparedness and how it can save lives

Chapter 8: The role of technology in earthquake response

- Overview of the role that technology plays in responding to earthquakes

- Discussion of the benefits and limitations of using technology in disaster response

Chapter 9: Public perception of earthquakes in Turkey

- Overview of the public's perception of earthquakes in Turkey
- Discussion of the impact that perception has on the response to earthquakes

Chapter 10: Conclusion

- Summary of the key points discussed in the book
- Final thoughts on the earthquake and its impact on Turkey.

Chapter 1

Introduction

Turkey is located at the crossroads of two major tectonic plates, the African Plate and the Eurasian Plate. This geographic location makes it one of the most seismically active countries in the world, with a history of devastating earthquakes.

The recent earthquake that struck the country was a powerful reminder of the destruction that earthquakes can bring. With its magnitude of 6.0, it caused widespread damage and injury, leaving many communities struggling to recover.

The significance of this earthquake extends far beyond the immediate damage it caused. It highlights the need for better earthquake preparedness and highlights the ongoing threat of earthquakes to the region. Understanding the causes and impacts of earthquakes, as well as the steps that can be taken to prepare for them, is essential for reducing their impact and preventing future losses.

Chapter 2

Causes of the Earthquake

Earthquakes are a result of the movement of tectonic plates beneath the Earth's surface. Turkey is located at the crossroads of two major tectonic plates, the African Plate and the Eurasian Plate, making it one of the most seismically active countries in the world.

Tectonic plates are massive slabs of the Earth's lithosphere, which is the outermost layer of the Earth consisting of the crust and the uppermost part of the mantle. The lithosphere is divided into several large plates, each moving independently and interacting with one another at plate boundaries.

In Turkey, the African Plate is moving northward and is slowly being forced under the Eurasian Plate, a process known as subduction. The movement of these plates creates friction and pressure along the boundary, causing the plates to become locked. Over time, the build-up of pressure and energy between the two plates becomes so great that it is eventually released in the form of an earthquake.

The science behind earthquakes is rooted in the study of geology, seismology, and plate tectonics. Earthquakes are caused by the release of energy stored in rocks within the Earth's crust. This energy is generated by the movement of tectonic plates and the friction that results from their movement. When the energy stored in these rocks exceeds their strength, they break and slip along a fault line, releasing the energy in the form of seismic waves.

Seismic waves are waves of energy that travel through the Earth's crust and can cause the ground to shake, which is what we experience as an earthquake. The strength and duration of an earthquake are determined by several factors, including the magnitude of the earthquake, the depth of the focus (the point within the Earth where the earthquake originates), and the proximity to populated areas.

In conclusion, earthquakes are a result of the movement of tectonic plates beneath the Earth's surface. Understanding the science behind earthquakes and how they are caused is critical to developing effective earthquake preparedness and response strategies. By studying the causes of earthquakes, we can better understand their impact and take steps to reduce their impact on communities and individuals.

Chapter 3

The Earthquake's Impact

The recent earthquake that struck Turkey caused widespread damage and injury, leaving many communities struggling to recover. The earthquake had a magnitude of 6.0, making it a significant event that impacted a wide area. The impact of the earthquake was felt across multiple cities and towns, with many buildings and infrastructure being damaged or destroyed.

The damage caused by the earthquake was extensive, with numerous buildings and structures collapsing or suffering significant damage. This included homes, schools, and businesses, many of which were left uninhabitable. The destruction of infrastructure such as roads, bridges, and power lines also had a significant impact, making it difficult for rescue and recovery efforts to be carried out.

The loss of life and injuries sustained as a result of the earthquake were also significant. According to official reports, several people were killed and many more were injured. The number of casualties was compounded by the fact that many buildings and structures were not adequately prepared to withstand an earthquake of this magnitude, resulting in widespread damage and collapse.

In the aftermath of the earthquake, rescue and recovery efforts were launched to help those who were affected. Emergency services and volunteers worked tirelessly to search for survivors, provide medical assistance to the injured, and help those who were displaced find temporary shelter. Despite these efforts, the impact of the earthquake was felt for many months, with communities and individuals still struggling to recover from the damage that was caused.

The impact of the earthquake serves as a reminder of the devastating consequences that can result from such events. The loss of life, injury, and damage to infrastructure and property are all significant, and it is essential that we work to better understand the impact of earthquakes and take steps to reduce their impact in the future. This includes improving building codes and earthquake preparedness measures, as well as investing in research and technology to better predict and respond to earthquakes.

In conclusion, the recent earthquake in Turkey had a significant impact on communities and individuals. The loss of life, injury, and damage to infrastructure and property were all significant, and it will take time for communities to fully recover from the event. It is our hope that by better understanding the impact of earthquakes, we can take steps to reduce their impact in the future and help communities and individuals to be better prepared for such events.

Chapter 4

Search and Rescue Efforts

In the aftermath of an earthquake, the role of emergency services is critical in responding to the disaster and providing assistance to those who are affected. The search and rescue efforts that are carried out in the aftermath of an earthquake are a crucial part of this response, as they help to locate and rescue survivors who may be trapped in the rubble of collapsed buildings.

In the case of the recent earthquake in Turkey, emergency services and volunteers worked tirelessly to search for survivors and provide medical assistance to the injured. Teams of rescue workers, including firefighters and medical personnel, were deployed to the affected areas to search through the rubble of collapsed buildings, using specialized equipment and techniques to locate and rescue survivors.

The search and rescue efforts were carried out using a combination of manual and mechanical methods, including the use of dogs, sonar equipment, and heavy machinery. The aim of these efforts was to locate survivors as quickly as possible and provide them with the medical assistance that they needed. In many cases, rescue workers were able to locate and extract survivors from the rubble, sometimes after several days of searching.

The search and rescue efforts that were carried out following the earthquake in Turkey were both complex and challenging, due to the widespread damage that was caused and the difficult conditions that rescue workers faced. Despite these challenges, the efforts of emergency services and volunteers helped to save many lives and provide crucial assistance to those who were affected by the disaster.

In conclusion, the search and rescue efforts that were carried out following the recent earthquake in Turkey were a critical part of the response to the disaster. The efforts of emergency services and volunteers helped to locate and rescue survivors, provide medical assistance to the injured, and support those who were affected by the earthquake. These efforts are a testament to the bravery and dedication of those who work in emergency services, and demonstrate the importance of having a well-prepared and effective response in place in the aftermath of a disaster.

Chapter 5

Providing Aid to Those Affected

In the aftermath of a disaster such as an earthquake, the provision of aid to those who have been affected is a crucial part of the response effort. This aid can take many forms, including medical assistance, food and shelter, and support for those who have lost their homes or loved ones.

In the case of the recent earthquake in Turkey, aid organizations and government agencies worked together to provide assistance to those who were affected. Aid organizations provided food, shelter, and medical assistance to those who were injured or displaced, while government agencies worked to coordinate the response effort and provide support to those who were affected.

The provision of aid in the aftermath of an earthquake is a complex and challenging process, due to the widespread damage that is caused and the difficult conditions that often exist in the affected areas. For example, the rubble from collapsed buildings can make it difficult to access affected areas, while limited infrastructure and resources can limit the ability of aid organizations to provide assistance.

Despite these challenges, the efforts of aid organizations and government agencies helped to provide crucial assistance to those who were affected by the earthquake in Turkey. By working together and leveraging their resources, these organizations were able to provide support and assistance to those who needed it most, helping to ease the suffering of those who were affected by the disaster.

In conclusion, the provision of aid in the aftermath of an earthquake is a critical part of the response effort, and is essential in helping to support those who have been affected. The efforts of aid organizations and government agencies play a crucial role in this process, and their work helps to ensure that those who are affected by the disaster receive the support and assistance that they need to recover.

Chapter 6

The Recovery Process

The aftermath of an earthquake can be a challenging and difficult time, as communities and individuals work to pick up the pieces and rebuild their lives. The recovery process can be long and complicated, but with the right support and resources, it is possible to overcome the obstacles and rebuild stronger and better than before.

The recovery process following the recent earthquake in Turkey will involve a number of different steps and challenges. One of the first steps will be to clear away the rubble and debris from the affected areas, so that reconstruction can begin. This will require heavy equipment and skilled workers, as well as careful planning and coordination.

Another important part of the recovery process will be to provide support and assistance to those who have been affected by the earthquake. This may include providing temporary housing, food and medical assistance, as well as helping people to access the resources and support that they need to get back on their feet.

In addition to these immediate needs, there will also be a need to rebuild the physical infrastructure of the affected communities. This may involve repairing damaged buildings, roads, and other important structures, as well as restoring essential services like power, water, and communication.

Despite the challenges that are inherent in the recovery process, it is important to remain optimistic and hopeful about the future. With the right support and resources, it is possible to overcome the obstacles and rebuild stronger and better than before. This may involve learning from the experience of the earthquake and incorporating new building standards and practices that can help to prevent future disasters.

In conclusion, the recovery process following an earthquake can be challenging, but with the right support and resources, it is possible to overcome the obstacles and rebuild stronger and better than before. By working together and providing support to those who have been affected, we can help to ensure that communities and individuals have the resources and support that they need to recover and rebuild.

Chapter 7

Preparing for Future Earthquakes

Earthquakes can strike at any time, without warning, and it is essential that individuals and communities are prepared for the possibility of a disaster. Preparing for earthquakes can help to save lives, reduce damage, and speed up the recovery process following an earthquake.

There are a number of steps that individuals and communities can take to prepare for earthquakes. For example, it is important to understand the risks associated with earthquakes in your area, so that you can take appropriate action to reduce your risk. This may include retrofitting your home or building, so that it is better able to withstand the impact of an earthquake, or developing an emergency preparedness plan that outlines what you will do in the event of a disaster.

Another important aspect of earthquake preparedness is being aware of the signs of an earthquake, and knowing what to do when one strikes. This may include learning how to "drop, cover, and hold on" to protect yourself during an earthquake, or knowing what to do if you are caught in an earthquake while you are in a building or a vehicle.

It is also important to understand the importance of being prepared for the aftermath of an earthquake, including having emergency supplies on hand, knowing how to access information about the disaster and its aftermath, and knowing how to get in touch with loved ones and family members.

In conclusion, preparing for earthquakes is an important aspect of disaster preparedness and response, and can help to save lives and reduce damage following a disaster. By taking the time to understand the risks associated with earthquakes, and taking the steps necessary to prepare, individuals and communities can be better equipped to handle the challenges and obstacles that may arise following an earthquake.

Chapter 8

The Role of Technology in Earthquake Response

In the aftermath of a natural disaster like an earthquake, the rapid and effective deployment of resources is critical to saving lives, reducing damage, and supporting the recovery process. Technology has increasingly become an important tool in responding to earthquakes, providing real-time information, coordination, and support to those affected by the disaster.

One of the key benefits of technology in earthquake response is the ability to quickly and accurately assess the extent of the damage. This can be done through the use of satellite imagery, unmanned aerial vehicles (UAVs), and other remote sensing technologies, which can provide real-time information about the location and extent of damage to buildings, roads, and other critical infrastructure.

Another important aspect of the role of technology in earthquake response is the ability to coordinate the efforts of emergency services and aid organizations. This can be done through the use of mobile and web-based technologies, such as incident management systems, that allow organizations to collaborate in real-time and respond more effectively to the needs of those affected by the disaster.

However, while technology can play an important role in earthquake response, it is also important to be aware of its limitations. For example, access to technology may be limited in the immediate aftermath of a disaster, due to power outages or other infrastructure damage. Additionally, technology is not always able to capture the full extent of the damage, as it may be limited by cloud cover or other environmental conditions.

In conclusion, technology plays an increasingly important role in earthquake response, providing real-time information, coordination, and support to those affected by the disaster. While there are certainly limitations to the use of technology in disaster response, it has the potential to make a significant difference in the outcome of a disaster, and to support the recovery process following an earthquake.

Chapter 9

Public Perception of Earthquakes in Turkey

In Turkey, earthquakes have been a frequent and devastating natural disaster for centuries. Despite this history, there is still much to be done in terms of educating the public about the dangers of earthquakes, and how to prepare for and respond to them. In this chapter, we will delve into the public's perception of earthquakes in Turkey and discuss the role that education and media play in shaping this perception.

One of the key factors affecting the public's perception of earthquakes is their level of education and awareness about these events. While some people may have a basic understanding of earthquakes, many others may not fully grasp the science behind them and how they occur. This can lead to confusion, fear, and even panic in the aftermath of an earthquake.

For example, people may not understand the importance of seeking shelter or evacuating the affected area during an earthquake. They may not know that the most dangerous place to be during an earthquake is inside a building, or that the best way to protect oneself is to drop, cover, and hold on. This lack of understanding can put people in harm's way, and make it more difficult for rescue workers to provide aid.

The media can also play a significant role in shaping the public's perception of earthquakes. In the aftermath of an earthquake, the media may report on the damage, the number of casualties, and the response efforts. This information can be critical for those who are directly impacted by the earthquake, as it can provide them with important updates and help them to make informed decisions about their safety.

However, the media can also contribute to misconceptions and misunderstandings about earthquakes. For example, they may present inaccurate or sensationalized information about the impact of earthquakes, or they may focus on the most dramatic aspects of the event without providing a full and balanced view of what has occurred. This type of coverage can lead to fear and panic, and can make it more difficult for rescue workers and aid organizations to do their job.

In order to support a more effective response to earthquakes, it is important to promote accurate and responsible media coverage of these events. This can be achieved by providing media outlets with accurate information about earthquakes and their impacts, and by encouraging them to present this information in a clear, concise, and non-sensationalized manner.

Another important factor in shaping the public's perception of earthquakes is the role of public agencies and aid organizations. These organizations can play a critical role in educating the public about earthquakes, and in promoting earthquake preparedness. For example, they can provide information on how to prepare for an earthquake, what to do during an earthquake, and how to respond in the aftermath of an earthquake.

In conclusion, the public's perception of earthquakes is a critical factor in determining how people respond to and prepare for these events. By increasing awareness and education about earthquakes, and by promoting accurate and responsible media coverage, we can help to reduce the risks and impacts of these disasters, and to support a more effective response in the aftermath of an earthquake.

Chapter 10

Conclusion

In this chapter, we will summarize the key points discussed throughout the book, and offer our final thoughts on the earthquake and its impact on Turkey. Earthquakes are a natural disaster that can have significant impacts on communities and the environment, and it is important that we are prepared to respond to them effectively.

Throughout this book, we have explored the causes of earthquakes, the impact they can have on communities, and the efforts that are made to respond to them. We have discussed the science behind earthquakes, the role that technology plays in responding to them, and the challenges and obstacles that must be overcome in order to recover from their effects.

In addition, we have looked at the public's perception of earthquakes in Turkey, and the importance of increasing awareness and education about these events. We have seen how the media can play a critical role in shaping the public's understanding of earthquakes, and how the public's perception can impact the response to these events.

Finally, we have explored the recovery process after an earthquake, and the importance of preparing for future earthquakes. We have seen the steps that can be taken to prepare for these events, and the benefits of being prepared for earthquakes.

In conclusion, earthquakes are a natural disaster that can have significant impacts on communities and the environment. However, by increasing awareness and education about these events, preparing for future earthquakes, and responding effectively to their impact, we can reduce their risks and impacts, and support a more effective recovery process. This book has aimed to provide a comprehensive understanding of earthquakes and their impact on Turkey, and to highlight the importance of preparing for and responding to these events.